The
Rise
of
Barack
Obama

Photographs
and text by

Pete Souza

TRIUMPH
BOOKS

This book is available in quantity at special
discounts for your group or organization.
For further information, contact:

TRIUMPH BOOKS
542 South Dearborn Street
Suite 750
Chicago, Illinois 60605
(312) 939-3330
Fax (312) 663-3557

ISBN 978-1-60078-163-6
Printed in U.S.A.

Produced by Pete Souza

Photographs edited by Pete Souza
and Julie Elman

Designed by Julie Elman

Production coordinated by Jill Donovan,
Wagner/Donovan Design

"Dream big dreams."

— BARACK OBAMA

Sen. Barack Obama works in his office on Capitol Hill in 2005.

Introduction

"Glad to have you," Barack Obama said, shaking my hand in a relaxed manner. In a few hours, he would be sworn in as the junior U.S. Senator from Illinois — 99th out of 100 in seniority. I was meeting him on this unseasonably warm January 2005 morning at his Washington hotel, ready to tag along during his first official day in the nation's capital.

At the time, I was the Washington-based national photographer for the *Chicago Tribune,* Sen. Obama's hometown newspaper. My *Tribune* colleague, political correspondent Jeff Zeleny, had proposed a series for the paper on the senator's first year in office and asked me if I was interested in taking part. ("Of course!" I replied.)

Ever since his stirring keynote address at the 2004 Democratic Convention, Sen. Obama had been touted as an up-and-coming star of his party. Ironically, I didn't see or hear his speech. But I certainly had read about Barack Obama and knew he was more than just the self-mocking "skinny guy with a funny name."

Several weeks before Sen. Obama was sworn in, Zeleny and I met with the senator's communications director, Robert Gibbs, to outline our plan. Gibbs promised cooperation, though pinning him down on the logistics later became a challenge. I think he thought I would go away, but I pestered him with e-mails and phone calls for the next couple of weeks, and Gibbs came through with the access he'd promised.

I tried not to be a nuisance to Sen. Obama on that first day, but I also tried to set a standard for the level of behind-the-scenes access I wanted to maintain. Photographs of politicians in public settings are innumerable, but the images that often become timeless are the quiet moments captured in more intimate settings. These are also the photographs that, to me, reveal the true character of a person.

Sen. Obama's family accompanied him to most of the ceremonial activities on his first day. This presented some terrific opportunities to candidly photograph him interacting with his two young daughters, Malia, then 6, and Sasha, then 3. The loving relationship that the girls have with their father is obvious from those pictures.

A few days after the swearing-in ceremony, Jeff Zeleny and I headed to Springfield, Ill., where Sen. Obama officially opened his new field office. The place was jam-packed. After the senator addressed the crowd, supporters descended on him seeking handshakes and autographs. At one point, Sen. Obama spotted me trailing him, and turning back towards me said, "Hey, I really like those pictures you took of me with my kids." He asked me for some prints and I followed through with his request the following week.

What struck me early on was how easily Sen. Obama conducted himself while I was photographing him. He went about his business; I went about mine. Even on that very first day, I thought the senator had a certain presence that I have not witnessed in a lot of

Sen. Obama walks unrecognized down a Moscow sidewalk in 2005.

politicians. "He's a natural," I told friends.

I have worked in Washington for 25 years, covering presidents, senators and representatives, both in public and private settings. Barack Obama is truly one of a kind. His intelligence is obvious but not off-putting, his concern is genuine, and if the occasion warrants, he can give as inspirational a speech as any politician I've ever seen.

There is also something else: Early into that first year, I began to believe that I was photographing a future president of the United States, and that my pictures might become an historic look at the rise of Sen. Obama's political career. That may sound like an easy statement to make now, but that's really how I felt at the time. And it certainly affected how I

approached my photographic coverage of the senator during the next two-and-a-half years.

I even used this thought process as a means to gain behind-the-scenes access to the senator. "This is for history," I'd say to the senator's communications director, when making requests. I'm sure he knew what I meant, though we never openly discussed it.

Having worked as an official White House photographer for President Ronald Reagan and having covered numerous presidential campaigns of both Democratic and Republican nominees, I have a keen sense of what life becomes like for politicians who reach that plateau. Hundreds of media descend on such a person, the Secret Service takes control of security, and it becomes difficult for journalists

Sen. Obama opens Nelson Mandela's former prison cell in South Africa in 2006.

to make photographs that look genuine.

Throughout 2005 and 2006, I thought very consciously about making photographs that were timeless and that would have contextual value in the future. My motivation went way beyond merely meeting the demands of a newspaper's limited space. Even while I was making these photographs two and three years ago, I imagined that you would be looking at these photographs *now*, in the context of where Sen. Obama is today.

I wanted you to see the drab, basement office (page 24) that every freshman senator endures during their first few months to show how far and how fast this particular senator has risen to power. I wanted you to see how easily Sen. Obama was able to walk unnoticed on a Moscow sidewalk (above left) in 2005. I wanted you to see the symbolic gesture of the only African-American in the U.S. Senate opening the former prison cell door of Nelson Mandela (above) in 2006. And I wanted you to see the certitude on Sen. Obama's face backstage seconds before he announced he was running for the presidency (page 123) in early 2007.

My coverage of Sen. Obama came to a self-imposed halt in the summer of 2007, when I resigned from the *Tribune* to begin teaching photojournalism at Ohio University. I felt my job was done: I had documented the rise of Barack Obama. The masses had already descended on the man likely to become the Democratic nominee for president of the United States.

— *Pete Souza*

Welcome to Washington

When Barack Obama first arrived in Washington, nearly every media outlet wanted access to him. But most of the cameras and reporters went away after his first couple of days in the U.S. Senate. That certainly made it easier for me to work.

The challenge now was in photographing the routine. The senator's family returned to Chicago and with them went the wonderful moments that occurred with his daughters Malia (pictured at right) and Sasha. By contrast, the working life of a U.S. senator is not that exciting. But keeping history in the back of my mind, I made sure I was making pictures that would be interesting to future viewers.

I also noticed an unusual dichotomy at play: though Sen. Obama was somewhat of a rock star in public settings, his mantra for that first year was to keep a low profile. Nowhere was that more evident than when he joined the Congressional Black Caucus in a meeting with President George W. Bush at the White House in January 2005. When the group held a press conference afterwards, Sen. Obama stood far in the back (page 30), shunning the cameras and dozens of reporters.

It was also interesting to watch people react to Sen. Obama in public settings. Supporters exhibited genuine excitement as they reached to shake his hand or give him a hug or ask for his autograph. Early on, when signing books for youngsters, the senator would use the salutation, "Dream big dreams."

Every Thursday morning, Sen. Obama and the senior senator from Illinois, Dick Durbin, would host "coffee with constituents." Anyone from Illinois visiting the nation's capital was invited to attend and participate in the question-and-answer session (page 26). With the Senate Democrats now in the majority, Sen. Durbin had become the second most powerful senator in the United States. Before one of the Thursday sessions, I overheard a couple of Illinois constituents talking about how excited they were to meet Sen. Obama.

"Who's the other senator from Illinois?" one of them asked me. I could only chuckle.

Sen. Obama participates in a ceremonial swearing-in (above) with members of the Congressional Black Caucus in January 2005. Sasha Obama (right) responds to television cameras as the Obama family greets Vice President Dick Cheney before the official swearing-in.

Sen. Obama and aides listen during a meeting in his office on his first day in the U.S. Senate.

Sen. Obama helps (left) his daughter Sasha avoid a puddle as he walks with his wife, Michelle, and their other daughter Malia to a reception in his honor at the Library of Congress on the day he was sworn in as a U.S. Senator. An affectionate Sasha (above) and Malia interrupt their father during a break for lunch.

"I stand here today, grateful for the diversity of my heritage, aware that my parents' dreams live on in my precious daughters. I stand here knowing that my story is part of the larger American story, that I owe a debt to all of those who came before me, and that, in no other country on earth, is my story even possible."

— BARACK OBAMA
2004 Democratic Convention keynote address

Sen. Obama and his daughter Malia inspect a statue of James Madison at the Library of Congress before a reception in the senator's honor.

In January 2005, during his first trip back to Illinois after becoming a member of the Senate, Sen. Obama answers questions during a town hall meeting in Waukegan (above) and meets with reporters (right) following a similar event in Lockport.

Sen. Obama receives a hug while greeting members of the audience following a town hall meeting in Illinois. Even during this first series of constituent gatherings, Sen. Obama faced overflowing crowds and had people converge on him whenever an event concluded.

Sen. Obama makes his entrance (above) during an open house at his new office in Springfield, Ill. Following a town hall meeting in Waukegan, Ill. (right), Sen. Obama signs posters made for the occasion.

Sen. Obama listens during a meeting in his sparse, temporary office in the basement of a Senate building in Washington, D.C. Ninety-ninth in seniority (out of 100 senators), Sen. Obama spent the first few months of his term housed in this location until he was moved to a permanent space in the Hart Senate Office Building.

During a weekly meeting on Capitol Hill with Illinois constituents visiting the nation's capital, Sen. Obama reacts as Sen. Dick Durbin (D-Ill.) mentions his colleague's rock-star status. Though Sen. Durbin was, in effect, the second most powerful Democrat in the Senate, more visitors were enamored by the hype surrounding Sen. Obama.

Sen. Obama listens (left) during a Senate hearing on Capitol Hill. He jokes with some of his Democratic colleagues (above) on the Senate Foreign Relations Committee prior to the start of a hearing. Left to right are Senators John Kerry (D-Mass.), Bill Nelson (D-Fla.), Joe Biden (D-Del.) and Christopher Dodd (D-Conn.).

During a press conference held by the Congressional Black Caucus after a White House meeting with President Bush in January 2005, Sen. Obama keeps a low profile, standing behind most members.

"We are here because we believe that all men are created equal, and that we are all connected to each other as one people. And we need to say that more. And say it again. And keep saying it."

— BARACK OBAMA
at the 65th birthday celebration of John Lewis

Holding hands with Coretta Scott King, Sen. Obama and others sing "We Shall Overcome" at Rep. John Lewis' 65th birthday celebration in Atlanta, Ga., in February 2005. Left to right: Sen. Obama, Mrs. King, Rep. Lewis, Ethel Kennedy and Kenny Leon.

(Following pages) Sen. Obama and President Bush attend a dedication ceremony at the Abraham Lincoln Presidential Library and Museum in Springfield, Ill., in April 2005. Also pictured, left to right, Sen. Dick Durbin, Rep. Ray LaHood (R-Ill.), Rep. J. Dennis Hastert (R-Ill.), Speaker of the House, Richard Norton Smith and First Lady Laura Bush.

Sen. Obama
waits to speak
at the Lincoln
Museum dedication
ceremony.

"And as that man called once upon the better angels of our nature, so is he calling still, across the ages, to summon some measure of that character, his character, in each of us, today."

— BARACK OBAMA
at the Lincoln Museum dedication

During the Lincoln Museum dedication, Abraham Lincoln impersonators wait for the cue to make their appearance.

A freshman abroad

In August 2005, Barack Obama traveled with a congressional delegation (CODEL) on a weeklong trip to inspect former nuclear weapons sites across the former Soviet Union. It was his first trip abroad as a U.S. Senator.

I was the lone photographer to accompany him on the trip.

Sen. Obama, then 44, was essentially an understudy on the trip to Sen. Richard Lugar, 73, a Republican from Indiana, and the chairman of the Senate Foreign Relations Committee.

Not long after arriving in Moscow, Sen. Obama took a walking tour of Red Square (pictured at right). No one recognized him as he viewed the Kremlin, Lenin's tomb, and the iconic St. Basil's Cathedral.

During the weapons inspection tour, Sen. Lugar was the seasoned veteran who was well known to his hosts. Sen. Obama was an unknown. "I very much feel like the novice and pupil," he told my colleague Jeff Zeleny for an article in the *Chicago Tribune*.

Sen. Obama is virtually unnoticed during a walking tour near Red Square in Moscow, Russia. Jeff Zeleny, at the time a *Chicago Tribune* reporter, is the man peeking through the group of tourists at right.

All eyes are on Sen. Obama (left) during a meeting aboard a military plane transporting a congressional delegation to Russia, Ukraine and Azerbaijan to inspect former nuclear weapons sites. Sen. Richard Lugar (R-Ind.), to the right of Sen. Obama, led the trip. Sen. Obama walks through the shell of a dismantled SS-24 nuclear missile (above) in Perm, Russia.

Sen. Obama inspects the
remnants of destroyed nuclear
missiles in Perm, Russia.

After the inspection tour ended in Perm, the congressional delegation was detained for three hours when Russian officials (top) insisted the CODEL didn't have permission to fly out of their country from the Perm airport to Ukraine. During the wait, Sen. Obama talks with an aide (right) and then catches some sleep (above). The detention made international news, albeit briefly, and the Russians finally allowed the CODEL to depart by saying there had been a miscommunication.

Sen. Obama, seated at right, meets
with Sen. Lugar and members of
the congressional delegation at an
airport lounge in Kiev, Ukraine.

Sen. Obama bows respectfully after a meeting with
Ukrainian President Viktor Yushchenko in Kiev.

Dr. Lyudmyla Tretyakova, chief of a pathogen laboratory, answers a question from Sen. Obama (left) during a tour of the Central Sanitary Epidemiological Station in Kiev. Test tubes containing anthrax and plague bacteria (above) were shown to Sen. Obama and Sen. Lugar.

Sen. Obama views
dismantled conventional
weapons at a destruction
plant in Donetsk, Ukraine.

Sen. Obama and a congressional delegation disembark from a U.S. military plane in Baku, Azerbaijan.

(Following pages) Sen. Obama attends a breakfast meeting in Baku.

All microphones point
toward Sen. Lugar
during a press conference held
in Baku, Azerbaijan.

With a poster of former Azerbaijani President Heydar Aliyev in the background, Sen. Obama listens during a mock interdiction in Baku.

Settling in

As his first year in the Senate was coming to a close, Barack Obama found himself front and center speaking to a crowd of journalists on Capitol Hill. The senator had been trying to keep a relatively low profile as a freshman, but Senate Minority Leader Harry Reid had tapped him to talk at a November 2005 press conference (left) and serve as the point person on ethics reform. More experienced Democratic senators were lined up behind him: from left, Hillary Clinton, Patty Murray, Mark Dayton, Barbara Boxer, Dick Durbin, Debbie Stabenow, Harry Reid, Jim Jeffords, Chris Dodd and Carl Levin.

This happened to be the week when I had been given behind-the-scenes access to photograph Sen. Obama for a year-end report in the *Chicago Tribune*. For my purposes, any week would have been fine. I was more interested in capturing the little moments that happen in routine situations; I didn't necessarily need to be there for any public news events. But as I look at this picture now, it seems a prescient image of the near future: this freshman senator would soon become a leading voice for the Democratic Party.

Sen. Obama confers with aides as he descends a staircase en route to a Senate hearing (above) and then walks up the steps of the U.S. Capitol (right) on his way to the Senate floor for a vote.

"In a nation torn by war and divided against itself, he was able to look us in the eye and tell us that no matter how many cities burned with violence, no matter how persistent the poverty or the racism, no matter how far adrift America strayed, hope would come again."

— BARACK OBAMA
speaking about Robert F. Kennedy in 2005

Ethel Kennedy (left), widow of former Sen. Robert F. Kennedy who was assassinated in 1968 when running for president, reacts to an offhand quip from Sen. Obama prior to the Robert F. Kennedy Memorial Human Rights Award ceremony on Capitol Hill in 2005. Sen. Ted Kennedy had just greeted Obama and thanked him for agreeing to be the keynote speaker. Obama replied that when Ethel called, he couldn't say no. "I think he feels it," Mrs. Kennedy told the *Chicago Tribune* in 2005, comparing her husband's quest for social justice to Sen. Obama's. "He feels it just like Bobby did."

A pensive Sen. Obama listens during
a meeting in his office.

Sen. Obama meets (top) with his chief speechwriter Jon Favreau, right, and communications director Robert Gibbs, middle, in his office on Capitol Hill in 2005. His then-personal assistant, David Kast, is in the background. The senator joins his interns (right) for lunch.

Sen. Ken Salazar (D-Colo.) chats with Sen. Obama (top) on the Senate subway in 2005. The senator confers (left) with legislative director Chris Lu, left seated, and communications director Gibbs during an impromptu meeting in Lu's office.

Sen. Obama relaxes
in his Senate office in
2005. The painting on
the wall behind him
is of former U.S.
Supreme Court Justice
Thurgood Marshall.

A United Air Lines pilot (above) takes a snapshot of Sen. Obama with a flight attendant after arriving at O'Hare Airport in Chicago in 2005. Cell phone in hand (left), Sen. Obama wheels his bag through O'Hare.

Higher visibility

There was a noticeable difference in Sen. Obama's public visibility as he began his second year in Washington.

When the Democrats appeared at the Library of Congress in early 2006 to sign an ethics pledge, Senate Minority Leader Harry Reid had Sen. Obama standing by his side (right). Sen. Obama also co-sponsored a bill on lobbying reform with Sen. Russ Feingold (D-Wis.).

Sen. Obama's work on this bill led to an exchange of testy letters between him and Sen. John McCain. Sen. McCain dressed down Sen. Obama and, according to the Associated Press, accused him of "self-interested partisan posturing" and being "disingenuous," while Sen. Obama shot back and called Sen. McCain "cranky."

The two later shook hands and hugged in public, but their relationship today is said to remain prickly.

Nonetheless, when an immigration bill was working its way through the U.S. Senate in March 2006, the two senators appeared together at a news conference on Capitol Hill and showed no animosity in public.

HONEST LEADERS

Sen. Obama confers with Sen. John McCain (R-Ariz.) as senators prepared to discuss the immigration bill during a press conference at the U.S. Capitol in March 2006. In the foreground is Sen. Edward Kennedy (D-Mass.); in the background, right, is Sen. Joe Lieberman (D-Conn.).

Sen. Obama shakes hands across the table with Rep. Grace Napolitano (D-Calif.) after Democrats signed an ethics pledge at the Library of Congress in Washington, D.C. in January 2006. Obama and others attacked the Republicans on ethics and proposed an overhaul on lobbying regulations.

Return to Africa

Kenyans perched atop trees as they waited for the arrival of Barack Obama (at left). After touring a hospital in Kisumu, the senator and his wife, Michelle, headed to a mobile clinic to have a rapid HIV blood test. It was a symbolic gesture aimed at this continent ravaged by AIDS, to show the importance of getting tested. Outside, thousands had gathered in hopes of catching a glimpse of the senator.

Similar scenes occurred throughout Kenya in August 2006, when Sen. Obama returned to the country where his father was born. Thousands of people traveled to see him in the tiny village where his paternal grandmother still lives, for what was supposed to be a private visit.

He traveled to Kibera, considered the largest slum in Africa, and was greeted by thousands of Kenyans who flooded the narrow streets to hear him make brief remarks. A day later in Nairobi, a huge, overflow crowd congregated outside a university auditorium, where loudspeakers broadcast Sen. Obama's speech on government corruption that he was delivering inside.

The senator's trip to Africa began with a visit to Nelson Mandela's prison cell at Robben Island, South Africa, and ended with a family vacation to the Masai Mara wildlife reserve in Kenya.

In South Africa, Sen. Obama meets with Archbishop Emeritus
Desmond Tutu (left) in 2006. The senator tours Robben Island
(above) near Cape Town, South Africa.

The senator stands inside the cell on Robben Island where Nelson Mandela was imprisoned during apartheid. Mandela was in prison for 27 years, 18 of which were here on Robben Island.

In Khayelitsha Township, South Africa, Sen. Obama meets with Babalwa Mbono, 31 (left), who is HIV positive and works with patients as part of the "Mothers2Mothers" program at a hospital that treats AIDS patients. A young boy (above) watches the senator conduct a press conference outside the hospital.

Sen. Obama meets with
well-wishers outside a restaurant
where he had a luncheon meeting
in Nairobi, Kenya.

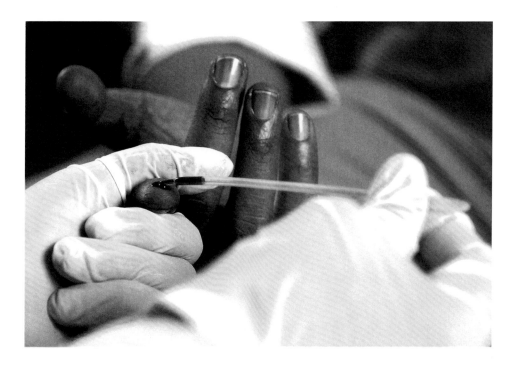

Kenyans shout for Sen. Obama (left) outside a health clinic in Kisumu, Kenya.
The senator's finger is pricked (above) for a rapid HIV blood test, intended to bring awareness
to the importance of being tested for AIDS.

An enthusiastic crowd welcomes the senator as he makes his way onto a makeshift stage outside a school named after him in his family's village in Kenya.

Sen. Obama snuggles with his daughter Sasha (above) at a CARE facility — partially funded by him — where elderly women care for their grandchildren who are AIDS orphans. With his grandmother in tow (right), the senator shouts at the surging crowd and media to keep back during a visit to his father's village in Kenya.

Sen. Obama addresses
an impromptu crowd
that gathered outside
a meeting in Kibera,
considered the largest
slum in Africa.

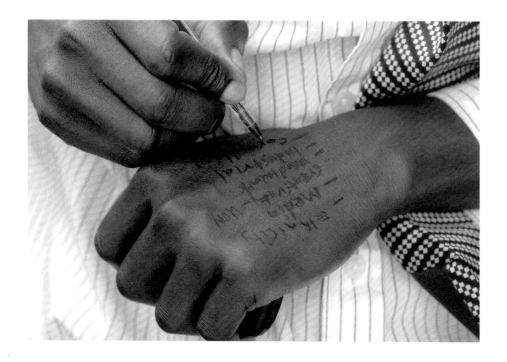

"In the end, if the people cannot trust their government to do the job for which it exists — to protect them and to promote their common welfare — all else is lost. And this is why the struggle against corruption is one of the great struggles of our time."

— BARACK OBAMA
during a speech at the University of Nairobi

A man listens to the senator's speech at the University of Nairobi (bottom left) while another jotted notes on his hand (top left). They were among the hundreds in the overflow crowd who couldn't fit inside the auditorium where the speech was being delivered. A policeman (above) holds back the crowd while also trying to catch a glimpse of Sen. Obama as he departed the scene.

(Following pages) Kenyans listen to the senator as he briefly addressed those waiting outside the University of Nairobi.

Sen. Obama, his daughters Malia and Sasha, his half sister Auma,
far right, and the daughter of a family friend, far left, watch a lion feast
on a wildebeest (above) during a safari at the Masai Mara wildlife
reserve in Kenya.

On the last leg of his Africa trip, Sen. Obama meets with Sudanese refugees at the Mile Refugee Camp near the town of Guereda, Chad.

Testing
the waters

The buzz had always been that someday the senator from Illinois would run for president of the United States. As 2006 came to a close, Sen. Obama fueled that rumor by paying a one-day visit to New Hampshire, home to the nation's first presidential primary.

Hundreds swarmed him during a book signing in Portsmouth. After visiting a coffee shop where he introduced himself to potential voters ("Hi, I'm Barack Obama"), he spoke to an energized, sold-out crowd at a Democratic fundraiser in Manchester. At a press conference before the fundraiser, he held court in front of more than 100 reporters (at right), who continued asking questions even after his spokesman called an end to the session.

In early 2007, the senator announced that he had formed a presidential exploratory committee. The next day, at a Senate Foreign Relations Committee hearing on Iraq, photographers focused their cameras on Sen. Obama instead of the witnesses who were testifying.

Two weeks later, in February 2007, a raucous student crowd welcomed him during a rally at George Mason University, just outside of Washington, D.C. Using Facebook, a social networking Web site that has more than 70 million active users, the young Obama supporters organized the rally.

Sen. Obama listens as Sen. Hillary Clinton (above) speaks at a Capitol Hill press conference after the minimum wage act passed the U.S. Senate in early 2007. At a Senate Foreign Relations Committee hearing on Iraq, photographers ignore the witnesses and instead focus their cameras (right) on Sen. Obama the day after he announced that he had formed a presidential exploratory committee.

Sen. Obama surveys the crowd at a Students for Barack Obama rally at George Mason University in Virginia in February 2007.

(Following pages) Lauren McGill and other students listen to the senator during the rally. Filmed by a "60 Minutes" crew, the event was held a week before Sen. Obama officially declared that he was running for president.

The night before his announcement speech,
Sen. Obama makes his way through a mob
scene as he arrives at his hotel in Springfield, Ill.

Presidential candidate

The weight of the moment was etched on his face. Barack Obama, the freshman senator from Illinois was about to announce to his constituents that he was running for president of the United States. Backstage (at left), his wife, Michelle, brushed specks of lint from his overcoat. Their daughters, Malia and Sasha, were dressed for the frigid temperatures that awaited them on this February morning at the Old State Capitol in Springfield, Ill.

Sen. Obama hugged Sasha and Malia, then kissed his wife. At one point, seemingly in prayer, he closed his eyes for a few seconds. As he was introduced to the crowd and the door flung open, a blast of cold air hit the family and staff. The campaign had officially begun. The now-presidential candidate made trips to Iowa, Chicago and New Hampshire as part of his "announcement tour."

Throughout the spring of 2007, I met up with Sen. Obama on the campaign trail, usually in New Hampshire, Iowa or South Carolina. All three states held early primaries or caucuses, and were crucial to any candidate's chance of winning the nomination.

That summer, I left the *Chicago Tribune* to become a photojournalism professor at Ohio University in Athens, Ohio. My coverage of Barack Obama had come to an end, I thought, but as it turned out, it was only put on hold.

Sen. Obama greets the crowd (above) at the Old State Capitol in Springfield, Ill., after announcing that he was running for president of the United States. Supporters brave frigid temperatures (right) to cheer him on.

(Following pages) People wait in line for a town hall meeting with the senator at a high school in Cedar Rapids, Iowa, in February 2007.

Michelle Obama and her two children, Malia and Sasha, sit behind the stage (above) as the senator speaks at Iowa State University in Ames, Iowa. The senator and Michelle wait to be introduced (right) at the rally.

A volunteer hands out campaign pins (left) in South Carolina. Campaign items are on display in New Hampshire (top) and Iowa (above).

The Democratic candidates for president appear on stage prior to a debate in Orangeburg, S.C., in April 2007. From left, Sen. Obama, Sen. Christopher Dodd (Conn.), former Sen. John Edwards, Rep. Dennis Kucinich (Ohio), Sen. Joe Biden (Del.), New Mexico Gov. Bill Richardson and Sen. Clinton.

Sen. Obama arrives (above) at a VFW in Dakota City, Iowa. At Rep. Jim Clyburn's annual fish fry (right) in Columbia, S.C., Sen. Obama and former Sen. Edwards converse before making remarks.

Sen. Obama (left) checks his Blackberry for messages before a fundraiser in Columbia, S.C., in February 2007. Backstage in a holding room (above), political advisor David Axelrod, left, confers with Sen. Obama before a press conference at Iowa State University in Ames.

Sen. Obama jokingly shows his hip-hop moves (above) for a group of high school students outside a diner in Peterborough, N.H. Audience members listen (left) to Sen. Obama during an event in Charleston, S.C.

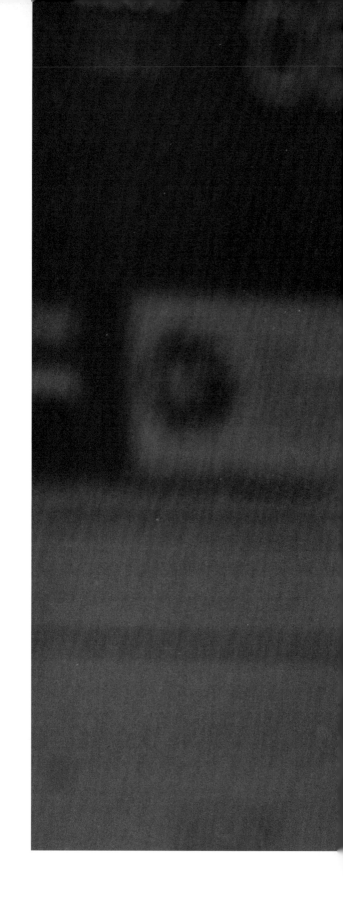

The senator speaks at a town hall rally in Keene, N.H.

During the announcement tour, people listen to Sen. Obama in Chicago (top), Springfield, Ill. (above) and Columbia, S.C. (right).

Sen. Obama consoles a woman (above) in Algona, Iowa, who told him about her 20-year-old son who had died in Iraq. "What can you say?" Sen. Obama told *The New York Times* afterwards. "This happens to me every single place I go." Sen. Obama mentioned the encounter the next day at a public rally. According to *The Times,* the woman had asked if her son's death was the result of a mistake by the government. "And I told her the service of our young men and women — the duty they show this country — that's never a mistake," he said. A young boy watches Sen. Obama (right) at a meet-the-candidate event in Fort Dodge, Iowa.

*"That's what satisfies me now,
I think — being useful to my
family and the people who elected
me, leaving behind a legacy that
will make our children's lives more
hopeful than our own."*

— BARACK OBAMA
from his book "The Audacity of Hope"

Following a 2007 campaign event in Iowa, Sen. Obama signs copies
of his books "The Audacity of Hope" and "Dreams from My Father."

The ascent continues

After watching the core of the presidential campaign from afar, I reconnected with Sen. Obama when he campaigned in Ohio and Pennsylvania in 2008.

"We've come a long way," one of his aides joked to me. Behind me stood dozens of photographers, hundreds of reporters, thousands of supporters and a bevy of Secret Service agents flanking Sen. Obama as he shook hands at the end of a rally in Columbus, Ohio.

In March, I rode with Sen. Obama on his bus as he made his way to a bowling alley in Altoona, Pa. (pictured at right with personal aide, Reggie Love). During his bus tour of the state, the senator made numerous OTR (off-the-record) stops between the scheduled campaign rallies and town hall meetings. (Most presidential candidates visit diners, restaurants, bars, and even bowling alleys, but do so unannounced.)

The senator also spoke on the Old Main lawn at Penn State University before a crowd of more than 20,000 people. When his remarks reached a crescendo, I noticed that some students had tears in their eyes. Hundreds of supporters surged forward, hands outstretched, as he worked the crowd. The junior senator from Illinois had become the Democratic front-runner for president of the United States.

CHICAGO WHITE SOX

LAST SEASON		AL RANK
BATTING AVG.	.246	Last
RUNS/GAME	4.3	Last
ON-BASE PCT.	.318	Last
HOME RUNS	190	2nd
LOWEST IN MLB		

U.S. Secret Service agents keep a close watch (above) as Sen. Obama lunches at Pat's, home of the famous Philly cheesesteak in Philadelphia, in April 2008. Members of the traveling press corps (left) work adjacent to the main event, where in the far background, Sen. Obama conducts a town hall meeting at Montgomery County Community College in Blue Bell, Pa.

With emotion in his voice, the senator delivers his campaign stump speech at a rally in Scranton, Pa.

Sen. Obama relaxes on his campaign plane (top) while talking with his wife, Michelle, as they flew from Philadelphia to Pittsburgh. Beer in hand (right), the senator toasts his tablemates at a bar in Bethlehem, Pa.

The senator tries his hand at bowling (top) in Altoona, Pa. He threw a couple of gutter balls before finally bowling a spare. At the Glider Diner in Scranton, Sen. Obama tries to engage Daniel Van Dusky (left) in conversation.

Penn State University students listen as Sen. Obama winds up his campaign speech on the Old Main lawn of the campus in March 2008.

Secret Service agents flank the senator as he shakes hands following his campaign speech at Penn State University before a crowd that was estimated to be more than 20,000 people.

Acknowledgments

First and foremost, I thank Barack Obama for allowing me to document the rise of his political career. I also owe thanks to Robert Gibbs, his communications director, whose trust in me made many of the pictures in this book possible. Others helpful on Sen. Obama's Senate and campaign staffs have been Tommy Vietor, Mark Lippert, David Kast, Dan Pfeiffer, Bill Burton, Jen Psaki, Katie Lillie, Samantha Tubman, Marvin Nicholson and Peter Weeks.

Most of the photographs printed here were originally taken on assignment for the *Chicago Tribune*, when I worked as the national photographer based in their Washington, D.C., bureau. I had the good fortune of working alongside *Tribune* correspondent Jeff Zeleny, now with *The New York Times*, who proposed documenting Sen. Obama's first year in the Senate. Jeff and I also covered the senator on his trips to Eastern Europe and Africa.

I thank Torry Bruno, my former boss and the *Tribune's* assistant managing editor for photography, for his help and support in obtaining permission from the *Tribune* to use my photographs in this book. Others at the *Tribune* who I thank are Robin Daughtridge, Mike Tackett, Ann Marie Lipinski, Jim Warren, Randy Weisman and the other *Tribune* reporters that I worked with on coverage of Sen. Obama: Mike Dorning, John McCormick, Dave Mendell, Christi Parsons and Mark Silva.

I've had the pleasure of working with Julie Elman, who designed this book in record time and who has also been helpful for this project as a picture editor, copy editor and cheerleader. I also thank Jill Donovan of Wagner/Donovan Design in Chicago and my sister Amy Souza, who has saved me from many grammatical errors.

At Triumph Books, I thank the indefatigable Mitch Rogatz for making this book happen. Thanks also to Tom Bast and Don Gulbrandsen.

I teach at Ohio University's School of Visual Communication and I thank our director, Terry Eiler, and the entire faculty for their support.

THIS BOOK IS DEDICATED to my aunt, Jessie Piva, who was always one of my biggest fans. Whenever my photographs were published in a book or magazine, she would carry them to her weekly (all-day!) appointment at the hair salon so she could brag about her nephew to "the girls."

She called me immediately when she heard I was documenting Sen. Barack Obama. "Pete, send me some pictures of Obama!" Another time, she called to say she'd found a picture of Sen. Obama and me together in *Ebony* magazine. I laughed when I finally saw the picture, which in reality was a picture of Sen. Obama at a Sudanese refugee camp in Chad; I was a small figure in the distant background. But to her, it was a picture of the senator and me together.

Aunt Jessie passed away recently at the age of 90. I plan to deliver a copy of this book to her friends at the hair salon.